Real Girls:

Reflections

Kiana Clayborn, LMSW

Jessica Traylor, Ed.S.

Cover Art by Daniel Sergent

Printed in the United States of America

ISBN: 978-0-615-43246-5

Unless otherwise noted, Scripture quotations are from the Holy Bible, New International Version, copyright © 1973, 1978, 1984 by International Bible Society.

Visit us at http://www.realgirls.us

Email the authors at contact@realgirls.us

Dedication

Real Girls: Reflections is dedicated to young women and the adults who care about them.

Thank you to all the girls who have participated in Real Girls groups. Your honesty and courage have helped to teach other girls.

Thank you!

This book is recommended as a compliment to the group discussion guide - *Real Girls: Shifting Perceptions on Identity, Relationships, and the Media.*

Comments from past participants:

I learned...

- You should always be you and live in reality.
- You should do what you love and don't let anyone take that away from you.
- No one can make you do anything that you don't want to do because you have a powerful mind of your own.
- The best way to express yourself is to be you. You shouldn't want to be like someone else, you should want to be you.
- Different types of relationships (healthy and unhealthy).
- Models in magazines are airbrushed.
- Try to show the real you. Love who you are.

General Comments

- I liked talking about music lyrics and magazines.
- I liked being in a girls-only group because you can open up more than when guys are around.
- Be a real girl! Eat an Oreo!!
- Real girls can do anything.

CONTENTS

Introduction

This book is a tool to help you learn about yourself, your relationships, and the media. You can go through each page in order or skip around. The choice is yours.

You might have noticed that there are activities on many different topics that usually interest girls your age. These activities can be done alone, with a friend, or with an adult. Either way, the point is to help you learn more about yourself.

Each lesson includes suggested media resources. These may be video clips, songs, or websites related to the topics. You can use the media resources to learn more or to share what you have learned with a friend.

There are also bible-based activities and biblical resources. Each scripture is followed by questions to get you thinking about what these truths mean in your life. You may choose not to complete these activities if you or your family members are opposed to Christian beliefs. We, Kiana and Jessica, believe the Bible is true and provides guidance for our daily lives. It was our hope to offer this same sort of guidance to you.

Feel free to add your writing to the forum on our website www.realgirls.us.

Support System

Guiding Questions

1. Who knows you best?
2. Who do you look up to?
3. How can these people help you as you learn more about yourself, relationships, and media?

Support Systems

It is important to know that you have a support system. A support system is made of people in your life who can help you make good choices and feel good about yourself. Think about positive and supportive adults or friends in your life that you can trust and talk to when you need help or guidance.

List their names below.

_____

_____

_____

_____

_____

_____

Sometimes you need to be reminded of how awesome you are. The people you have listed above will all be great reminders for you.

Getting Support

Some people have a large support system, while others have a small number of close friends and family. In either case, there will be times when you need help or guidance and you do not know who to talk to or how to begin the conversation. Here are a few steps to follow:

1. Decide who you want to talk to.
2. Think about what is happening in your life and what you need that person to do for you.
3. Pick the right time & ask if they have time to talk.
4. Give as much information as you can.
5. Accept that their answers may not be what you wanted to hear.

What are some things in your life, now or in the future, that you think you would want to talk to someone about? _____

What types of support do you think you will need? _____

_____

Give examples of bad times to talk to someone. _____

_____

Give examples of good times to talk to someone. _____

_____

What will you do if their answer is not what you wanted to hear? _____

Real Me

Guiding Questions

1. Who are you? What makes you special?
2. How do you know how a young woman should think, talk, act, and dress?
3. How do your self-concept and media awareness impact your relationships and choices?

Self-Concept

Self-concept refers to how we view ourselves in relation to the world around us. Sometimes young women develop a negative self-concept, thinking they are not as good as others. Sometimes young women develop an inflated self-concept, thinking they are better than others. A positive, balanced self-concept will allow young women to recognize their strengths and weaknesses.

Answer the following questions:

What are your strengths? _____

What are your weaknesses? _____

What are your life goals? _____

Can you achieve those goals? _____

I am special because _____

Bonus – Ask someone close to you to answer those questions based on what they know about you.

Female Role Models

Girls are not born knowing who they are or how to be young ladies. Ideas about how to act, talk, and dress are learned from what we see around us and the expectations set for us. Think about a few women you know personally (mother, grandmother, sister, aunt, cousin, teacher, etc.). Think about what you have learned from them about what it means to be a young lady. List a few of those things below.

1.
2.
3.
4.
5.

Ask two or three women what it means to be a woman. Record their answers below.

1.
2.
3.

What do you think about their answers? Does anything surprise you? Do you agree with their answers?

_____

_____

_____

Media Messages

Research shows that false ideas about female beauty, body shapes, and limited gender stereotypes negatively affect young women. Media can include television shows, magazines, internet websites, music, video games, billboards, clothing store models, print and video ads, and movies. Many of the media descriptions of girls show them in limited roles focused on superficial beauty. We will explore this topic in detail during the next few lessons. For now, think about the following questions:

- What do you usually see girls and women doing in movies, music videos, advertisements, television shows, and video games? _____

  _____

- Do real girls and women do these things? _____
- Does media give you the whole picture? _____
- What is missing from media messages about girls and women? _____

You may not be able to answer all of these questions right now. As you watch TV, surf the web, or listen to music, begin to look for how girls and women are shown. Look for what they are doing, saying, and wearing. You may be surprised to find that media messages are not always the same as real life.

Biblical Womanhood

According to the bible, young women should be trustworthy, hardworking, intelligent, strong, compassionate, and wise (Proverbs 31: 10-31). Read this passage for yourself to gain a better understanding of the characteristics of a biblical woman.

In which of these areas do you excel? _____

Which area do you need to work on? _____

Are you a hard-worker who forgets to help those around you? Can you be trusted to do what is right? Do you need to rely on the experience of older women while you gain more wisdom? _____

_____

According to the bible, we are called to demonstrate inner beauty, rather than be obsessed with our outward appearance. Why do you think it would be important to work toward developing inner beauty? _____

_____

What are some of the downfalls of relying on outer beauty to determine your self-worth? _____

_____

There is nothing wrong with wearing makeup and taking care of your body, as long as you know that the most important part of you is on the inside.

Media Resources

You can use these resources for further thought and discussion with friends and family.

Videos (www.wingclips.com)

Akeelah and the Bee – Deepest Fear

- Dr. Larabee forces Akeelah to read an inspirational quote and then explain what it means to her.
- Discuss: What does this scene mean to you? Why would some people be afraid to succeed?

Phoebe in Wonderland – I'm Scared

- Phoebe learns from Miss Dodger that one day she will come to accept and love her individuality.
- Discuss: What does this scene mean to you? Is there something about you that makes you different or special? What does it mean to love yourself? Why do you think Phoebe says she is scared?

Nanny Diaries – Who Am I?

- While in an important job interview, Annie can't find the answer the question: Who is Annie Braddock?
- Discuss: Why is it important to know who you are? Who or what tells you who you are? How do you know which messages are correct?

Biblical Resources

Philippians 2:15 – so that you may become blameless and pure, children of God without fault in a crooked and depraved generation, in which you shine like stars in the universe

- What does Paul mean when he writes that we should be blameless and pure?
- Do you believe we live in a crooked and depraved generation? What makes you think that?
- Why do we need young women to "shine like stars?"
- How can you shine?

Jeremiah 1:5 - Before I formed you in the womb I knew you, before you were born I set you apart

- How does it feel to read that God knew you before you were born? Is that hard to believe?
- What were you set apart for?
- How would someone act if they believed they were created for a special purpose?

1st Peter2:9 - But you are a chosen generation, a royal priesthood, a holy nation, a peculiar people

- What does it mean to be a chosen generation?
- How can you encourage your peers to become the change that is needed at this time in history?
- Is it possible for girls your age to be holy and pure? Why or why not?

Lesson Reflections

What did you learn about self-concept and female role models? _____

_____

_____

_____

_____

_____

_____

_____

_____

_____

_____

_____

_____

_____

_____

_____

_____

_____

_____

_____

_____

_____

Self-Reflection

What did you learn about yourself?

_____

_____

_____

_____

_____

_____

_____

_____

_____

_____

_____

_____

_____

_____

_____

_____

_____

_____

_____

_____

_____

Media Messages

Guiding Questions

1. What is the purpose of media and marketing?
2. How important is media to you?
3. What impact does the media you watch or listen to have on your self-image and goals?

Media and Marketing

Young girls spend a large part of their waking hours watching or listening to messages from the media about how they should look, dress, think, and behave. According to the Kaiser Family Foundation, media use by youth has increased to almost eight hours a day. The majority of that time is spent watching television (4.5 hours), listening to music (2.5 hours), and using the computer (1.5 hours). The sole purpose of media is to sell or tell you something. Everything you read is an attempt to convince you to buy or believe something.

Answer the following questions:

Do you think you spend too much time watching TV, using the computer, or listening to music? _____

What do you think about teen magazines? _____

_____

Are pictures in magazines and on TV realistic? _____

Magazine Analysis

The next time you are at a store find a teen magazine and look through it. While you are turning pages, look at the titles of the articles, the products that are being advertised, and all of the pictures. What did you find?

- What products are being advertised? _____

  _____

  _____

- Based on the articles, what should girls your age be interested in and concerned about? _____

  _____

  _____

- What do these articles and advertisements say about girls? What would someone else think about girls, based on this magazine? _____

  _____

  _____

- What impact do these types of media messages have on girls? What impact do they have on society?

  _____

  _____

- What is your viewpoint? _____

  _____

  _____

  _____

"Evolution" of a Photo

Watch the "Evolution" video from Uniquely Me and Dove
(www.studio2b.org/lounge/games/uniquelyMe/main.html). If
this link does not work, you may find the video by
searching the internet for "Dove Evolution video." While
watching, pay attention to all the steps involved. The
beginning shows a real girl walking into the photo shoot
and the end is a billboard with "her" photo.
Write down the steps shown in the video.

    1.

    2.

    3.

    4.

    5.

    6.

What do you think about the computer changes to her
neck, eyes, hair, nose, etc.? _____

_____

The video text says "no wonder our perception of beauty
is distorted." What does this mean to you? _____

_____

_____

Look at the magazine again and see if you can find some
pictures that have been computer edited. Begin to look
at flawless skin (no pores?), perfect bodies, etc.

American Idols

The bible is very clear about the fact that Christians should not put any idol above God (Exodus 34:17 and Deuteronomy 4:16). Further reading reveals that an idol can be anything that you spend a lot of time thinking about or a lot of money trying to achieve. For many girls and women, the perfect look is their idol. For others, status or popularity is their idol. Consider the following questions to check yourself regarding the presence of idols in your life.

What do you spend most of your time thinking about?

_____

_____

What is something that, if you don't have it or can't get it, you are very unhappy? _____

_____

What do you spend most of your money on? _____

_____

What are you unwilling to give up, even if it means you will hurt yourself or someone else? _____

_____

When you locate idols in your life, you are encouraged to give them up. Some idols are easily given up, while others take time. The idea is that God is enough. He is seated in the highest place in your heart and mind.

Media Resources

Video

Penelope – Not Your Nose (www.wingclips.com)

- Penelope and her mother discuss how the imperfection that is her nose affects the possibility of finding a boyfriend.
- Discuss: What does this scene mean to you? Where do our ideas of beauty come from? What is real beauty? Is there any part of your body that you would like to change?

Audio

"Barbie Girl" by Aqua

- Discuss: What does this song say about girls? What does it mean to be a "Barbie girl?"

Internet

www.about-face.org – Advertising about girls and women

- Discuss: What do these advertisements imply about women and girls? How do the creators of this website deal with advertisements? What can you do about unrealistic or degrading images of girls?

www.medialit.org – Center for Media Literacy

- Explore the media analysis tools on this website

Biblical Resources

Deuteronomy 4:16 – so that you do not become corrupt and make for yourselves an idol, an image of any shape, whether formed like a man or a woman

- What does it mean for someone to become corrupt?
- How can a man or woman be an idol? Can friends or boyfriends be idols? What would that look like?
- What sort of idols do we have in our society?

Deuteronomy 7:25 – The images of their gods you are to burn in the fire. Do not covet the silver and gold on them, and do not take it for yourselves, or you will be ensnared by it, for it is detestable to the LORD your God.

- What does it mean to "covet" material things? How does media encourage us to covet what others have?
- Do you believe you can be ensnared (trapped) by material things?
- Can you think of a movie where the characters had to give up an image of an idol? (Lord of the Rings)

Daniel chapter 3 – King Nebuchadnezzar demands that all people bow down to the golden image he has created. Three Jews refuse to obey this command. They are thrown in the fiery furnace and rescued by God.

- How does this relate to peer-pressure to look or dress a certain way? What happens to those who do not conform to society's standards of beauty and fashion?

Lesson Reflections

What did you learn about media messages?

_____

_____

_____

_____

_____

_____

_____

_____

_____

_____

_____

_____

_____

_____

_____

_____

_____

_____

_____

_____

_____

_____

<u>Self-Reflection</u>

What did you learn about yourself?

_____

_____

_____

_____

_____

_____

_____

_____

_____

_____

_____

_____

_____

_____

_____

_____

_____

_____

_____

_____

Musical Messages

Guiding Questions

1. Do many girls your age use drugs or drink alcohol? Is this acceptable?
2. How often do popular songs talk about using drugs or drinking alcohol?
3. What impact does the media have on your ideas about the prevalence of drug and alcohol use?

Music's Content

Young girls today are surrounded by thousands of media messages each day. One in three popular songs contains explicit references to drug or alcohol use. This means that girls your age are receiving about 35 references to substance abuse for every hour of music they listen to. Considering this information, a majority of youth receive more than 100 messages every day about substance use and/or abuse.

Answer the following questions:

What is your favorite song? _____

Does that song talk about drugs or alcohol? _____

How many songs can you list that do not talk about drugs or alcohol? _____

_____

Theme Song

Think about all the songs you love to listen to. Pick one that you would call your "theme song." This song should represent you as you are now, or as you see yourself in the future.

- What song did you choose? _____
- Write out some of the lyrics from your song.

  _____

  _____

  _____

- Why did you choose this song? What does it mean to you? _____

  _____

- What does this song imply about girls? What would someone else think about girls, based on this song?

  _____

  _____

- What impact do these types of media messages have on girls? What impact do they have on society?

  _____

  _____

- What have you learned about yourself from analyzing this song? Do you still think this is your theme song?

  _____

Today's Popular Music

Listen to the radio, watch music videos, or use the computer to make a list of five of today's top songs.

   1.

   2.

   3.

   4.

   5.

What is the main point of each of these songs?

   1.

   2.

   3.

   4.

   5.

Chances are many of the songs talk about unhealthy relationships, fighting, using drugs, or drinking alcohol. Do you agree with the messages in these songs? _____
If you are like most girls, you find yourself repeating songs in your mind, like a broken record, without even thinking about it. Is this the kind of thing you want to think about all day every day? _____
If not, what can you do about it? _____

_____

What song has a positive message you would like to have playing in your mind? _____

Music as Ministry

In biblical times, being a musician meant being a holy servant of God (1st Chronicles 9:33). Musicians lived in the temple and were treated with honor (Nehemiah 10:39). Music in the bible is used in several ways. It is used to communicate with God (Psalms), worship God (1st Chronicles 6), bring joy (Nehemiah 12:27), and express emotions (Ephesians 5:19).

In what ways do we honor musicians today? _____

_____

How was music used in the bible? _____

_____

Music is still used for worship. Some examples could include the worship of the self, money, power, and sex. Give some examples of things that are worshiped in the music you listen to. _____

How do you use music to communicate with God? _____

_____

What influence does music have over your emotions?

_____

Identify one song that brings you joy. _____

Identify one song that makes you sad. _____

How are Christian musicians seen in our society? _____

_____

Media Resources

Video (www.wingclips.com)

Akeelah and the Bee – Words Change the World

- Frustrated that her spelling coach is making her read essays instead of memorizing words, Akeelah learns that it is the power of the words that matter.
- Discuss: What does this scene mean to you? Why are the words that we hear or speak important? Do you believe that words can change the world?

Madea's Family Reunion – Where You're Going

- After taking Madea's advice to study hard, Nikki is rewarded for her hard work with a "B' on her Algebra test.
- Discuss: What does this scene mean to you? How does your history impact your present and your future?

Audio

"I Am Not My Hair" by India Arie

- Discuss: What does she mean when she says "I am not your expectations?" What impact does this song have on the way you feel about yourself?

"Just a Girl" by No Doubt

- Discuss: What message does this song send about girls? Why would she "rather not" be a girl?

Biblical Resources

Deuteronomy 32:28-29 – They are a nation without sense, there is no discernment in them. If only they were wise and would understand this and discern what their end will be.

- To discern means to be able to tell the difference between right and wrong. Why is this important?
- What happens when you listen to all messages without discernment?

Hebrews 4:12 – For the word of God is living and active. Sharper than any double-edged sword, it penetrates even to dividing soul and spirit, joints and marrow; it judges the thoughts and attitudes of the heart.

- What happens when we apply the word of God to the music we listen to?
- Do your favorite songs align with the bible?
- How is popular music helpful in exploring, or judging, the thoughts and attitudes of your heart?

Proverbs 3:13 - Blessed is the man who finds wisdom, the man who gains understanding.

- In what ways can analyzing music help you gain wisdom? Can we learn from music?
- Are some songs more helpful than others?
- Is it wise to listen to songs with hurtful messages?

Lesson Reflections

What did you learn about musical messages?

_____

_____

_____

_____

_____

_____

_____

_____

_____

_____

_____

_____

_____

_____

_____

_____

_____

_____

_____

_____

_____

Self-Reflection

What did you learn about yourself?

_____

_____

_____

_____

_____

_____

_____

_____

_____

_____

_____

_____

_____

_____

_____

_____

_____

_____

_____

_____

Media Stereotypes

Guiding Questions

1. What is a stereotype?
2. How are different groups of people treated differently in school and society?
3. What impact does the media have on your ideas about different groups of people?

Stereotypes and Discrimination

Stereotypes are set ideas about someone or something. They are mental shortcuts. You can quickly put people into boxes based on how they look, talk, dress, or act. You may assume you know how all "teenage mothers" are because you know one or have seen some examples on TV. Stereotypes become harmful when they lead to discrimination, which is treating someone different based on a category, rather than based on their individuality.

Answer the following questions:

What are some common stereotyped groups at your school? _____

Are some stereotypes true? Explain. _____

_____

What do you do when you find yourself stereotyping people? _____

Gender Differences in Media

Think about the different ways that females and males are seen on TV and in music. Women and girls are often shown as passive and powerless. Females are usually shown in the house, laughing, talking, or watching what others are doing. Men and boys, on the other hand, are often shown as independent, active, and powerful. Males are usually shown outside, building, working, or fighting.

- What is an example of a show that shows females in this limited role? _____
- What is an example of a show that shows females doing different things? _____
- Why do you think media shows females and males in this way? _____
- How would you change the way girls and women are shown on TV and in music? _____
  _____
- How are media messages about females connected to low self-esteem, depression, and eating disorders?
  _____
  _____
- What would happen if young girls were shown all the different things females can do? _____
  _____

Stereotypes

Think about the groups of people on the list below. Write the first thing that comes to mind. You may write things that other people think or say about that group.

- Overweight girls - _____
- Private school students - _____
- Smart girls - _____
- Black girls - _____
- Divorced parents - _____
- Teenage moms - _____
- Teachers - _____
- Poor girls - _____
- Girl Scouts - _____
- Christians - _____
- Doctors - _____
- Cheerleaders - _____
- Disabled girls - _____

It was probably easy for you to think of stereotypes for all those groups of people. Most people naturally think in groups and categories. The challenge is to catch yourself when you are thinking of a person in a stereotypical way and change your thoughts. What could you say to yourself when you are thinking in stereotypes? _____

_____

_____

Biblical Equality

The bible makes it very clear that all human beings are created in the image and likeness of God (Genesis 1:26-27). God loved the world so much that He sent Jesus to lay down His life for us (John 3:16). The "world" obviously includes all ethnic groups. God does not show favoritism (Deuteronomy 10:17; Acts 10:34; Romans 2:11; Ephesians 6:9), and neither should we. Instead, we are to love our neighbors as ourselves (James 2:8). How would you compare favoritism and discrimination?

_____

_____

What do you think about the way your church treats groups of people? _____

_____

In church, are some people treated better than others? If so, how? _____

_____

What are the problems with favoritism and discrimination? _____

_____

What are some ways you can show that you care about someone who seems different from you? _____

_____

_____

Media Resources

Video (www.wingclips.com)

Crash – One More Time

- The director is pressured to shoot another take of a scene, so as to perpetuate racial stereotypes.
- Discuss: What are your thoughts about this video? Do you think this happens?

The Boy in the Striped Pajamas – Nice Jew

- Bruno and his sister receive misinformation from a tutor about Jewish people.
- Discuss: Are stereotypes ever entirely true? Why would people want to perpetuate stereotypes about themselves or others?

Crash – Blind Fear

- Anthony and Peter discuss how the poor service they received at a restaurant was due to racial stereotypes.
- Discuss: What are your thoughts about this video? Is it possible to be racist against people of your own race? Is it possible to be sexist against other females?

Internet

www.media-awareness.ca/english/issues/stereotyping/ - media stereotypes and the impact on young people

Biblical Resources

Genesis 1:27 – So God created man in his own image, in the image of God he created him; male and female he created them.

- If God created us all in His image, then what do you think God thinks about stereotypes?

Romans 12:2 – Do not conform any longer to the pattern of this world, but be transformed by the renewing of your mind. Then you will be able to test and approve what God's will is – His good, pleasing, and perfect will.

- What does it mean to "conform to the pattern of this world?" How does that relate to stereotypes?
- How can you renew your mind to rid it of stereotypes? Could you remind yourself that we are all created in God's image?

Galatians 3:28 – There is neither Jew nor Greek, free nor slave, male nor female, for you are all one in Christ Jesus.

- If we are all one, who is hurt when we apply stereotypes to other people? Are we all impacted?
- Do you think males should have more privileges than females? How does this work in our society?
- What does it mean to be "in Christ Jesus?" What does this say about those who are not "in Christ Jesus?"

Lesson Reflections

What did you learn about stereotypes?

_____

_____

_____

_____

_____

_____

_____

_____

_____

_____

_____

_____

_____

_____

_____

_____

_____

_____

_____

Self-Reflection

What did you learn about yourself?

_____

_____

_____

_____

_____

_____

_____

_____

_____

_____

_____

_____

_____

_____

_____

_____

_____

_____

_____

_____

Real Talk

Guiding Questions

1. Do you think words are powerful?
2. What type of words do you use to describe yourself?
3. Does how you think about yourself impact the choices you make?

Affirmations/Positive Self-Talk

Affirmations are positive beliefs or facts that you have about yourself. When you use affirmations and talk positively to and about yourself, you build up your self-esteem. Having a positive view of who you are, and believing it, may help you handle situations in life better and help you make positive life choices. As a young woman it is important to feel good about who you are because there are so many influences that may tell you that you are not pretty, special, smart, and beautiful. You have to believe that you are all of this and more.

Answer the following question:

When you think about yourself, is it mostly positive or negative? Give some examples of things you say to yourself. _____

_____

Positive Characteristics

What is one positive characteristic that you have?

_____

Did you have to think hard to answer the question above? If you answered yes, please explain why.

_____

_____

How do you (or can you) use this characteristic to make the world a better place? _____

_____

Complete the following affirmations:

I am special because_____

I love my _____

I am good at _____

I am still working on _____

One day I will _____

I have so many great qualities, like_____

_____

Create your own affirmations below:

_____

_____

_____

Bonus- Ask someone close to you to answer those questions based on what they think about you.

Media Messages

The media can play a huge role in the things a young girl says to herself. Young girls today consume media on so many different levels: TV, music, magazines and social networks, just to name a few. Many girls may begin to look at themselves in a different way based on how media says girls are, or should be. Some girls look at media and all they see are thin girls with long, flowing hair and fashion designer clothing. The same girl may now think negatively of herself because she can't afford those clothes or make herself look that way. This is just an example of how media may influence a young girl's thoughts about herself and the world around her.

- What does the media tell you about yourself? I should be..._____

- Do you feel good about yourself after you watch television, read magazines, and listen to music? _____

- What activities make you feel good about yourself?

  _____

The next time you watch television, read a magazine, or listen to music pay attention to how you feel about yourself afterwards. Come back to this question to see if your answer changed or remained the same. You may be surprised to find out how much media can influence the way you think and feel about yourself.

Biblical Thoughts

According to the bible, you are a royal priesthood, a chosen generation (1st Peter 2:9). It is also important to know that the bible says that life and death is in the power of the tongue (Proverbs 18:21). Read these two passages for yourself to gain a better understanding of the way you should think about yourself and the type of words you should use to speak about yourself.

Do you believe that you are someone of great value? ___ How can your words impact your generation - this chosen generation? _____

Give examples of how you can use words to bring life?

   1.

   2.

According to the bible, we should think of ourselves as God thinks of us and not think of ourselves how the world may see us. We should be proud of who we are since we are made in the image of God. Why do you think it is important to see yourself as God sees you?

_____

Hopefully after completing this section you now have a better understanding of how important it is to speak positive words over your life and to think positive thoughts instead of negative thoughts about yourself.

Media Resources

Video (www.wingclips.com)

Gifted Hands – You Can Do This

- When her son begins to doubt his ability to perform a complex procedure, she encourages him that he can accomplish anything he sets his mind to.
- Discuss: Who in your life encourages you? What does she mean by "you've just gotta see beyond what you can see?"

An Angel for May – Not Possible

- Tom regrets saying some hurtful things to his mom and realizes that he can't go back and change it.
- Discuss: Have you ever said something you wish you could take back? What can you do to make positive decisions moving forward?

Audio

"Six Feet Tall" by Never Say Never

- Discuss: What do you think this song is about? What does it mean to be "as tall as your heart will let you be?" How could the world make you seem small?

Internet

www.girlshealth.gov – Information about bullying, relationships, and feelings

Biblical Resources

Deuteronomy 11:18-19 – Fix these words of mine in your hearts and minds; tie them as symbols on your hands and bind them on your foreheads. Teach them to your children, talking about them when you sit at home and when you walk along the road, when you lie down and when you get up.

- Why is it important to continually talk and think about the words of God?
- In what ways do you keep God's word in your heart and mind on a daily basis?
- What opportunities do you have to talk about God with your family and friends?

Proverbs 18:21 – The tongue has the power of life and death, and those who love it will eat its fruit.

- How can the tongue bring life? Death?

Philippians 4:8 – Finally, brothers, whatever is true, whatever is noble, whatever is right, whatever is pure, whatever is lovely, whatever is admirable—if anything is excellent or praiseworthy—think about such things.

- What do you spend more time talking about, positive things or negative things?
- How can you make more of an effort to think and talk about things that are true, right, pure, and lovely?

Lesson Reflections

What did you learn about communication and self-talk?

_____

_____

_____

_____

_____

_____

_____

_____

_____

_____

_____

_____

_____

_____

_____

_____

_____

_____

_____

Self-Reflection

What did you learn about yourself?

_____

_____

_____

_____

_____

_____

_____

_____

_____

_____

_____

_____

_____

_____

_____

_____

_____

_____

_____

_____

_____

_____

_____

Real Power

Guiding Questions

1. Do you believe that you are powerful?
2. What can you control?
3. What can you not control?

Power/Control

Many girls spend a great deal of time worrying about things they cannot control, such as parents, teachers, and rules. It is important to realize that the only person you can control is yourself. This is a key principal. It determines how you mange friendships, decisions, goals, and many other life situations. Once you realize that you are responsible for your actions and what you do, you may be able to make better life choices, which may lead to a more productive and successful life.

Answer the following questions:

If you could change one thing about your life, what would it be? _____

Do you ever find yourself trying to control things that you really cannot control? Give an example. _____

_____

How would life change if you only focused on what you can control? _____

What can you control?

It is important to recognize what you can control in life. Once you recognize this you will be able to make healthier decisions and save time from worrying about things that you cannot change. When you spend so much energy thinking and complaining about things that you cannot control you don't have time to focus on the things about yourself that you can change or improve. View the list below and circle the items that you control.

Natural Disaster   **Going to Jail**

Having Sex   **Joining a Gang**

Cheating   **Your School**

Family   **What Others Think of You**

Friends   **Using Alcohol**

Grades   **Your Future Goals**

Using Drugs

You Control You

It may be surprising to know that you can only control things that deal with you. From the list above you can control grades, future goals, using drugs or alcohol, having sex, and joining a gang - all by making positive decisions. All these things are based on your choices. This is why it is so important to make the right decisions.

What can you not control?

Now that you recognize the things you can control, looking at the same list, underline the things that you cannot control. How do you feel about the things you cannot control? _____

_____

_____

In what areas have you tried to control things that are outside your power? _____

Once you realize the things you cannot control, you will be better able to focus on the things you can control. This will help you to make wiser choices and healthier decisions. You will be free to explore all of the things that you can do, which will help you recognize how special you really are.

How would your life be different if you spent more time thinking about the things you can control? _____

_____

How would you grade yourself on knowing what you can and cannot control? _____

Bonus In your free time think about things that are not listed on the list above and add things to the list. Once you add more things to the list compare how many things you can control to how many things you can not control. The results may surprise you.

Biblical Power

According to the bible, God is the source of your power (Ephesians 3:20-21). This scripture states, "now unto him who is able to do immeasurably more than all we ask or imagine, according to his power that is at work in us." This lets you know that you have the power of God in you; that you are powerful. Knowing that you have the power of God in you will help you make choices that will help you reach your destiny and fulfill your future dreams. If you do not believe that you are powerful and that you have a purpose, you may let other people influence you to make bad choices that lead to negative consequences. Give an example of a time when you have been pressured by friends to make negative choices? _____

How did you feel about the choices you made? _____

_____

Now that you know that you have the power to make good choices and not give in to negative peer pressure, how do you feel? _____

What do you think it means to have the "power of God in you?" _____

What will you use your power for? What is your purpose? _____

Remember you have power and purpose!!

Media Resources

Video (www.wingclips.com)

The Great Debaters – Righteous Mind

- Melvin educates his students about a slave owner's method of controlling his slaves. His strategy was to "keep the slave physically strong but psychologically weak and dependent on the slave owner."
- Discuss: What do you think about this video? How does this relate to the topic of sexual harassment? What impact does sexual harassment have on girls?

When Zachary Beaver Came to Town – I Dare You

- Toby takes Cody up on a dare to climb the water tower and ends up in some real trouble.
- Discuss: What could he have done or said to avoid getting himself in that situation? Do your friends ever talk you into things that get you in trouble? How can you do what is right and keep your friends?

Audio

"Respect" by Aretha Franklin

- Discuss: How are power and respect related?

Internet

http://mychoice2wait.org/refusal.html - Abstinence-based refusal skills

Biblical Resources

Philippians 4:13 – I can do everything through Him who gives me strength.

- Who is it that gives the strength to do everything?
- What things, activities, or people renew your strength?

2 Corinthians 12:20 – That is why, for Christ's sake, I delight in weaknesses, in insults, in hardships, in persecutions, in difficulties. For when I am weak, then I am strong.

- How does this scripture relate to peer pressure?

Proverbs 24:5-6 – A wise man has great power, and a man of knowledge increases strength; for waging war. you need guidance, and for victory many advisers

- What does it mean to be wise?
- How can you gain wisdom and knowledge?
- What is the relationship between guidance and becoming a wise woman?

Ephesians 3:20 – Now to him who is able to do immeasurably more than all we ask or imagine, according to his power that is at work within us.

- What would happen if you allowed God to work through you to do more than you ask or imagine?
- How are you blocking God's work in and through you?

Lesson Reflections

What did you learn about power and control?

_____

_____

_____

_____

_____

_____

_____

_____

_____

_____

_____

_____

_____

_____

_____

_____

_____

_____

_____

Self-Reflection

What did you learn about yourself?

_____

_____

_____

_____

_____

_____

_____

_____

_____

_____

_____

_____

_____

_____

_____

_____

_____

_____

_____

_____

Healthy Relationships

Guiding Questions

1. What qualities does a true friend display?
2. How do you know when a friendship is positive?
3. Do you think you deserve to be treated with respect?

Healthy Relationships

In a healthy relationship each person feels valued and respected. Healthy relationships make both people feel good about who they are. Sometimes girls experience unhealthy relationships with people who may treat them badly and make them feel like they do not have any special qualities. It is important for girls to know that they deserve to have healthy relationships and that they do not have to settle for unhealthy relationships.

Answer the following questions:

Why is it important to choose friendships that make you feel good about who you are? _____

_____

What does respect mean to you? _____

Do you deserve to be treated with respect? What would that look like? _____

_____

Wise Women

Many girls may not know what a healthy relationship looks like because they may have never experienced it for themselves or they may not know anyone who has a healthy relationship. Think about a few women you know personally. Think about how they interact with their husbands, children, parents, friends, or boyfriends. List a few of your observations below.

1.
2.
3.
4.
5.

Ask two or three women how they would describe a healthy relationship. Record their answers below.

1.
2.
3.

What do you think about their answers? Do they surprise you? How do their responses compare with your answers above? _____

_____

_____

_____

_____

Media Messages

Many girls may get their idea of what a relationship is by watching television shows and listening to music. One of the problems with this is that many popular television shows do not display positive examples of healthy relationships. The best selling music of today often has lyrics that disrespect women and portray them in a negative way in relationships.

- Can you think of a television show or song that displays women in unhealthy relationships? Give an example. _____

- Can you think of a television show or song that displays women in healthy relationships? Give an example. _____

- How are men portrayed in the media? _____

_____

- How has the media shaped your ideas about what a relationship should be like? _____

_____

_____

Bonus - When you have free time, watch television and list the number of healthy relationships you see and then list the number of unhealthy relationships you see. Compare each list and review the results.

Biblical Relationships

The bible says that you should not be unequally yoked
with unbelievers (2nd Corinthians 6:14). We are also
instructed to encourage and live in peace with one
another (2nd Corinthians 13:11). Having similar beliefs
and a positive interaction are important parts of biblical
relationships. Read these passages for yourself to gain a
better understanding of the type of relationships that
God says you should have.

What does it mean to be equally yoked? _____

_____

Do you believe it is important to be friends with people
who have similar interests as you? _____
Why does the type of friends you have affect you?

_____

_____

According to the bible, we should lift each other up,
rather than tear each other down. Why do you think it is
important be involved in relationships where both people
feel encouraged and built up? _____

_____

_____

Which healthy relationships in your life provide
encouragement and support? _____

<u>Healthy Relationships Resources</u>

Video (www.wingclips.com)

Diary of A Mad Black Woman – Get Even

- After being shot and crippled, Charles was deserted by his new family and friends with no one to care for him but his ex-wife Helen, who he had spent years abusing and abandoned.
- Discuss: What do you think about this video? Who has the power in this video clip? What types of abuse do you see in this video?

Diary of A Mad Black Woman – Don't Be Like Me

- As payback for years of abuse, Helen has been mistreating her now-crippled ex-husband. Realizing the extent of the hurt he caused her, Charles urges her not to be like him.
- Discuss: What do you think about this video? Was it right for Helen to mistreat Charles?

Audio

"Fighter" by Christina Aguilera

- Discuss: What kind of situation is she talking about that made her stronger? Have you ever felt like you were to blame for someone else's bad choices?

Internet

www.loveisrespect.org – Teen dating abuse information

Biblical Resources

2 Corinthians 6:14 – Do not be yoked together with unbelievers. For what do righteousness and wickedness have in common? Or what fellowship can light have with darkness?

- What are some ways you could be "yoked together" with unbelievers?
- How could an unhealthy relationship prevent you from shining your light in the world?

2 Corinthians 13:11 – Finally, brothers and sisters, rejoice! Strive for full restoration, encourage one another, be of one mind, live in peace. And the God of love and peace will be with you.

- What does it mean to "encourage one another?"
- How can you use the relationships in your life to encourage others? What about the power of words?

Psalm 5:11 – But let all who take refuge in you be glad; let them ever sing for joy. Spread your protection over them, that those who love your name may rejoice in you.

- How does taking refuge in God help you in having healthy relationships?
- Does knowing this truth help you forgive others?

Lesson Reflections

What did you learn about healthy relationships?

_____

_____

_____

_____

_____

_____

_____

_____

_____

_____

_____

_____

_____

_____

_____

_____

_____

_____

_____

_____

_____

Self-Reflection

What did you learn about yourself?

_____

_____

_____

_____

_____

_____

_____

_____

_____

_____

_____

_____

_____

_____

_____

_____

_____

_____

_____

_____

Appendix Contents

Appendix A

Real Girls Pre-Survey

Please complete this survey. It contains questions about your view of yourself, media, and your relationships.

Background

Age: ___   Grade: ___

Mother's Education: _____   Father's Education: _____

Live with: __mother only; __father only; __both parents; __other

Typical grades: reading: A, B, C, D, F; math: A, B, C, D, F

Media Literacy

How many **hours** do you spend listening to or watching the following media sources **each day**?

__television; __radio; __CD player/iPod; __Internet

How many hours do you spend talking to family and/or friends (in person, not on the phone/text/email)? ____

What is your favorite TV show? _____

What is your favorite magazine? _____

What is your favorite movie? _____

What is your favorite website? _____

What is your favorite song? _____

What is your favorite video game? _____

What is your favorite book? _____

Self-Concept

How often are you physically active? ___minutes/day

Do you believe that you are over weight? __yes; __no

Are you currently trying to lose weight? __yes; __no

    If yes, how? __exercise; __diet pills; __fasting;

    __laxatives; __vomiting; __reduced calories

What do you worry about? __being pressured to have sex;

__having friends; __fitting in; __being pretty enough;

__being smart enough; __graduating from high school

Do you have a boyfriend? __yes; __no

    If yes, how old is he? ___

    Time spent together each week? ___hours

Are your friends sexually active? __yes; __some; __no

Do your friends drink alcohol? __yes; __some; __no

Do your friends use tobacco? __yes; __some; __no

Do your friends use drugs? __yes; __some; __no

Healthy Relationship

How do people treat each other in a healthy relationship?

_____

_____

_____

Please write True or False for the following items.

__It is against my values to have sex before I am married.

__It is against one or both of my parents' values for me to have sex before I am married.

__Teens who have been dating for a long time should have sex if they want to.

Please circle the response that is most like you.

I am happy with who I am.

>Never   Sometimes   Often Always

My friends are smarter or prettier than I am.

>Never   Sometimes   Often Always

I want to look like the girls in magazines.

>Never   Sometimes   Often Always

I compare myself to fashion models.

>Never   Sometimes   Often Always

Women in the media seem like real women.

>Never   Sometimes   Often Always

I let people take advantage of me.

>Never   Sometimes   Often Always

Appendix B

Real Girls Post-Survey

Please complete this survey. It contains questions about your view of yourself, media, and your relationships.

Background

Age: ____   Grade: ____

Mother's Education: _____   Father's Education: _____

Live with: __mother only; __father only; __both parents; __other

Typical grades: reading: A, B, C, D, F; math: A, B, C, D, F

Media Literacy

How many **hours** do you spend listening to or watching the following media sources **each day**?

__television; __radio; __CD player/iPod; __Internet

How many hours do you spend talking to family and/or friends (in person, not on the phone/text/email)? ____

What is your favorite TV show? _____

What is your favorite magazine? _____

What is your favorite movie? _____

What is your favorite website? _____

What is your favorite song? _____

What is your favorite video game? _____

What is your favorite book? _____

Self-Concept

How often are you physically active? ___minutes/day

Do you believe that you are over weight? __yes; __no

Are you currently trying to lose weight? __yes; __no

> If yes, how? __exercise; __diet pills; __fasting;
>
> __laxatives; __vomiting; __reduced calories

What do you worry about? __being pressured to have sex;

__having friends; __fitting in; __being pretty enough;

__being smart enough; __graduating from high school

Do you have a boyfriend? __yes; __no

> If yes, how old is he? ___
>
> Time spent together each week? ___hours

Are your friends sexually active? __yes; __some; __no

Do your friends drink alcohol? __yes; __some; __no

Do your friends use tobacco? __yes; __some; __no

Do your friends use drugs? __yes; __some; __no

Healthy Relationship

How do people treat each other in a healthy relationship?

_____

_____

_____

Please write True or False for the following items.

__It is against my values to have sex before I am married.

__It is against one or both of my parents' values for me to have sex before I am married.

__Teens who have been dating for a long time should have sex if they want to.

Please circle the response that is most like you.

I am happy with who I am.

       Never   Sometimes   Often Always

My friends are smarter or prettier than I am.

       Never   Sometimes   Often Always

I want to look like the girls in magazines.

       Never   Sometimes   Often Always

I compare myself to fashion models.

       Never   Sometimes   Often Always

Women in the media seem like real women.

       Never   Sometimes   Often Always

I let people take advantage of me.

       Never   Sometimes   Often Always

Final Self-Reflection

What did you learn while working through this book?

_____

_____

_____

_____

_____

_____

_____

_____

_____

_____

_____

_____

_____

_____

_____

_____

_____

_____

_____

_____

Appendix C

Love the real me or not?

If you look at a situation from more than one angle you can begin to see that things may look different from a different perspective. The same is true for you! In the stars below, write down things you don't like about your appearance. Then, next to each one, spin the "bad" thing into a good thing by thinking about how it might actually be helpful or good and why you should embrace it.

Appendix D

Real or Reel

Directions: Think about a television show you have watched that contains a lot of stereotypes.

TV Program Watched:

1. What stereotypes did you see in this show?

2. List a comment or action that illustrated stereotypical thinking.

3. Do you feel that television and media as a whole has an impact on our attitudes and beliefs?

Appendix E

Real People

Have you ever seen or experienced discrimination? When you see the categories below, please list the first message that comes to mind.

An Overweight Girl:

A Poor Girl:

A Teenage Mother:

A Girl Who Attends Private School:

What can you do to when you hear or see people being discriminated against?

Appendix F

Real Conversations

- Can you I cheat from your test because I didn't study?
- You have to tell the teacher that you ruined the textbook, not me.
- I want to borrow you blue shirt to wear to the school party.
- You know, your hair would really look better the other way, you should change it.
- I need to borrow your new sneakers; they will look perfect with my new jeans. I promise I won't ruin them.
- I need to take your car this weekend to go to work.
- Your friend dresses weird; you should stop hanging out with her.

Three Communication Styles

Aggressive: Expressing feelings in a way that violates the rights of others.

Passive: The failure to express needs, opinions, wants.

Assertive: Communicating what you want in a clear, respectful manner.

Appendix G

Real Situations

What would you do? #1

Your friend asks you to come to her house and help her study but what she didn't tell you is that her parents are away on vacation and when you arrive at her home she is having a party instead with alcohol. Which communication style would you use to express your feelings?

What would you do? #2

Your friend says she needs to borrow your new laptop to complete a school project that the each of you were given months ago and the project is due in one week. She says that she's been so busy that she hasn't had time to go to the library and use the computers. However, you know that she has been hanging out with her boyfriend almost every day and shopping at the mall with friends after school instead of working on the project. Which communication style would you use to express your feelings?

What would you do? #3

Your boyfriend has been asking you every day during class to leave school early and go hang out at a mutual friend's house. You know that your parents expect you to stay in school and come straight home when school is over. You know if you tell your boyfriend no, he may get upset. Which communication style would you use to express your feelings?

What would you do? #4

Create your own real situation...

Appendix H

Attitude

by: Charles Swindoll

The longer I live, the more I realize the impact of **attitude** on life. **Attitude**, to me, is more important than facts. It is more important than the past, than education, than money, than circumstances, than failures, than successes, than what other people think or say or do. It is more important than appearance, giftedness or skill. It will make or break a company... a church... a home.

The remarkable thing is we have a choice every day regarding the **attitude** we will embrace for that day. We cannot change our past... we cannot change the fact that people will act in a certain way. We cannot change the inevitable. The only thing we can do is play on the one string we have, and that is our **attitude**... I am convinced that life is *10% what happens to me and 90% how I react to it.*

And so it is with you...
we are in charge of our **attitudes**.

Appendix I

Real Control

Natural Disaster

Having Sex

Cheating

Family

Friends

Grades

Using Drugs

Going to Jail

Joining a Gang

Your School

What Others Think of You

Using Alcohol

Your Future Goals

Appendix J

Power to Say No

Know how you feel ahead of time.

Be firm and repeat what was said.

Be honest.

Speak only for yourself.

Discuss the consequences.

Separate the situation from the person.

Suggest an alternative.

Walk away from the situation.

Appendix K

Boundary Scenarios

Boundary-Crossing Behavior

- When Cheryl walked to class a group of boys whistled at her and it made her feel uncomfortable.
- Ruth keeps texting Christopher asking if he wants to have sex with her. Christopher has a girlfriend and has told Ruth on more than one occasion that he doesn't want to be with her.
- Thomas teased Susan while she was in gym class about her body shape.
- When Sean is at football practice, a group of girls rate how many muscles he has. Sean was so embarrassed.
- Michael never respects the boundaries of the girls in his class. He always gets really close to them and they are always uncomfortable.
- Jack tells Sandra that he will only help her with her project if she has sex with him.

Type of Boundary

- Inappropriate Physical contact
- Non-Consensual sexual advances
- Requests for sexual favors
- Inappropriate Verbal language

About the Authors

Jessica Traylor has extensive experience and training in youth development, group facilitation, program planning, culturally relevant teaching practices, statistical research, data analysis, parent engagement, and staff development. Mrs. Traylor was a featured presenter at national conferences, including: The National Youth at Risk Conference; The National Association of Social Workers Conference, Georgia Chapter. Jessica earned a B.S. in Psychology with a minor in Sociology from Georgia State University, followed by a M.Ed. and Ed.S in School Psychology from Georgia Southern University. Mrs. Traylor began her career in education as a Special Education Teacher. Currently, Jessica is a School Psychologist in Central Georgia. Jessica resides in Milner, GA with her husband and two children.

Kiana Clayborn has practiced as a Licensed Master Social Worker in both New York and Georgia. Her practice areas include school social work, case management, advocacy, program planning, youth development, group work, parent engagement, and staff development. Ms. Clayborn has been a featured presenter at national conferences, including: The National Youth At Risk Conference and The National Association of Social Workers Conference, Georgia Chapter. Kiana received both her B.A. degree in Sociology and her M.S.W. degree in Social Welfare from the State University of New York at Stony Brook. Ms. Clayborn began her career as a Social Work Case Manager in Preventive Services. Currently, she is a School Social Worker in Central Georgia.